Escape from NAZI BERLIN

Contents

Steck Vaughn™

A Harcourt Achieve Imprint

www.Steck-Vaughn.com
1-800-531-5015

How would you feel if your parents sent you to live in another country? What if it was for your own safety? My name is Hans. My parents sent me far away and it saved my life.

You'll understand why if you think about these ideas first.

Big Ideas

- Adolph Hitler led the Nazis to power in Germany in 1933. The Nazis hated Jews.

- By 1935, German Jews had lost all of their basic rights.

- November 9, 1938, is called *Kristallnacht*, or "The Night of Broken Glass." More than 1,100 temples—Jewish places of worship—were burned that night. Jews were killed or arrested across Germany.

- The Nazis sent millions of Jews to prison camps. More than six million Jews were put to death.

- Through the help of many people, thousands of Jewish children fled Germany during this period. They sought safety in other countries, including the United States.

It was November 9, 1938. Fourteen-year-old Rachel Werner lived in Germany with her family. She had a happy life. Then, the "Night of Broken Glass" began.

Papa, why are they doing this? You must stop them!

Be quiet.

Or they will kill us.

A man named Adolph Hitler ruled Germany. Most Germans joined his **Nazi** party. The Nazis hated anyone who was not exactly like them. Hitler and the Nazis were **anti-Semitic**—they especially hated Jews.

Heil Hitler!

Show me your papers. Are you a Jew?

Anti-Semitic **propaganda** was everywhere! Jews were treated like animals—or worse—by the Nazis.

Jews were not even safe in their own homes.

Come with me!

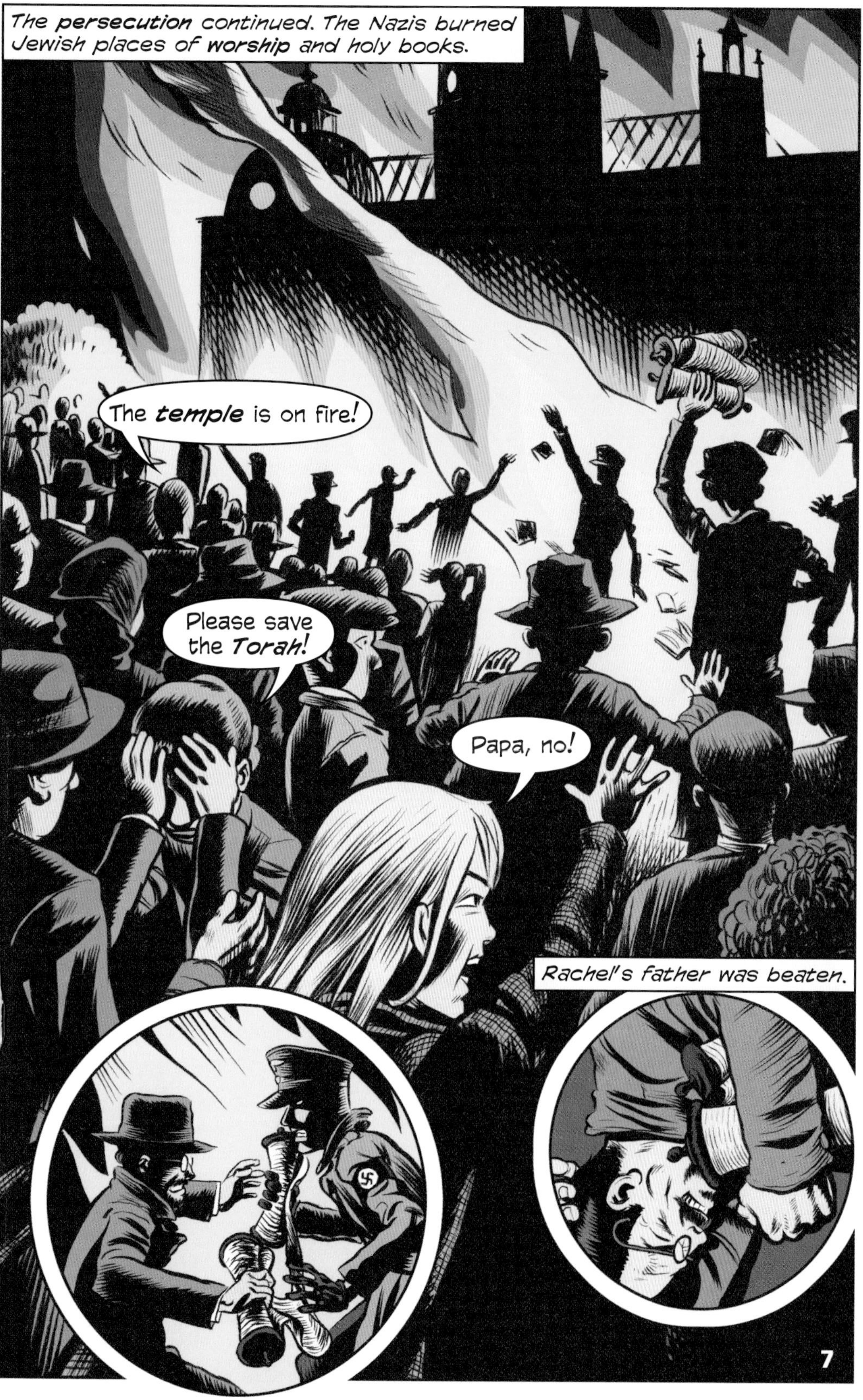
The **persecution** continued. The Nazis burned Jewish places of **worship** and holy books.
The *temple* is on fire!
Please save the *Torah*!
Papa, no!
Rachel's father was beaten.

Three days later, the children came home early.

Later that night, the children hear their parents talking.

The next morning, the decision is made.

Yolan is a very old friend. She is risking a great deal to help us.

Berlin is no longer safe.

You must go live with Yolan in Holland.

You will *portray* yourselves as Dutch *peasants*. Do not get *separated*.

Yes, Papa.

We will find you soon.

Keep your chin up, Sophie.

I don't want to go.

Here is Yolan. You will live with her until it is safe to come home.

Would you like some Dutch chocolate?

The train stopped at the border. Nazi police called *Gestapo* were looking for Jews.

Sophie, you must call this woman Mama. Do you understand?

Show me your papers.

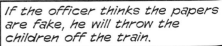

If the officer thinks the papers are fake, he will throw the children off the train.

If he thinks they are Jewish, he may kill them.

Heil Hitler.

Heil Hitler.

Rachel, Hans, and Sophie lived in Holland for a year.

They went to school.

They made friends.

But they were always careful.

And they waited for the day they could go home.

11

On May 10, 1940, the Nazis marched into Holland.

Wake up! We must leave.

There is a train to France. I will take you there.

Where is Sophie?

Sophie is sick. She will stay here with me.

NO!

I promised Papa we would stay together.

Many children will be hiding on the train. When you arrive, go to the *safe house*.

Thank you for everything.

You must go.

STOP!

The Nazis must have *invaded* France.

We must get to the safe house.

Or we will be shot.

13

KNOCK KNOCK

Yolan sent us.

The Nazis run France now. You must go to America.

My aunt and uncle live in America.

What are you writing?

Dates. Places. I'm trying to figure out where the Nazis will attack next.

March 15, 1939
Czechoslovakia

September 1, 1939
Poland

April 9, 1940
Denmark
and Norway

May 10, 1940
Holland, Belgium
France

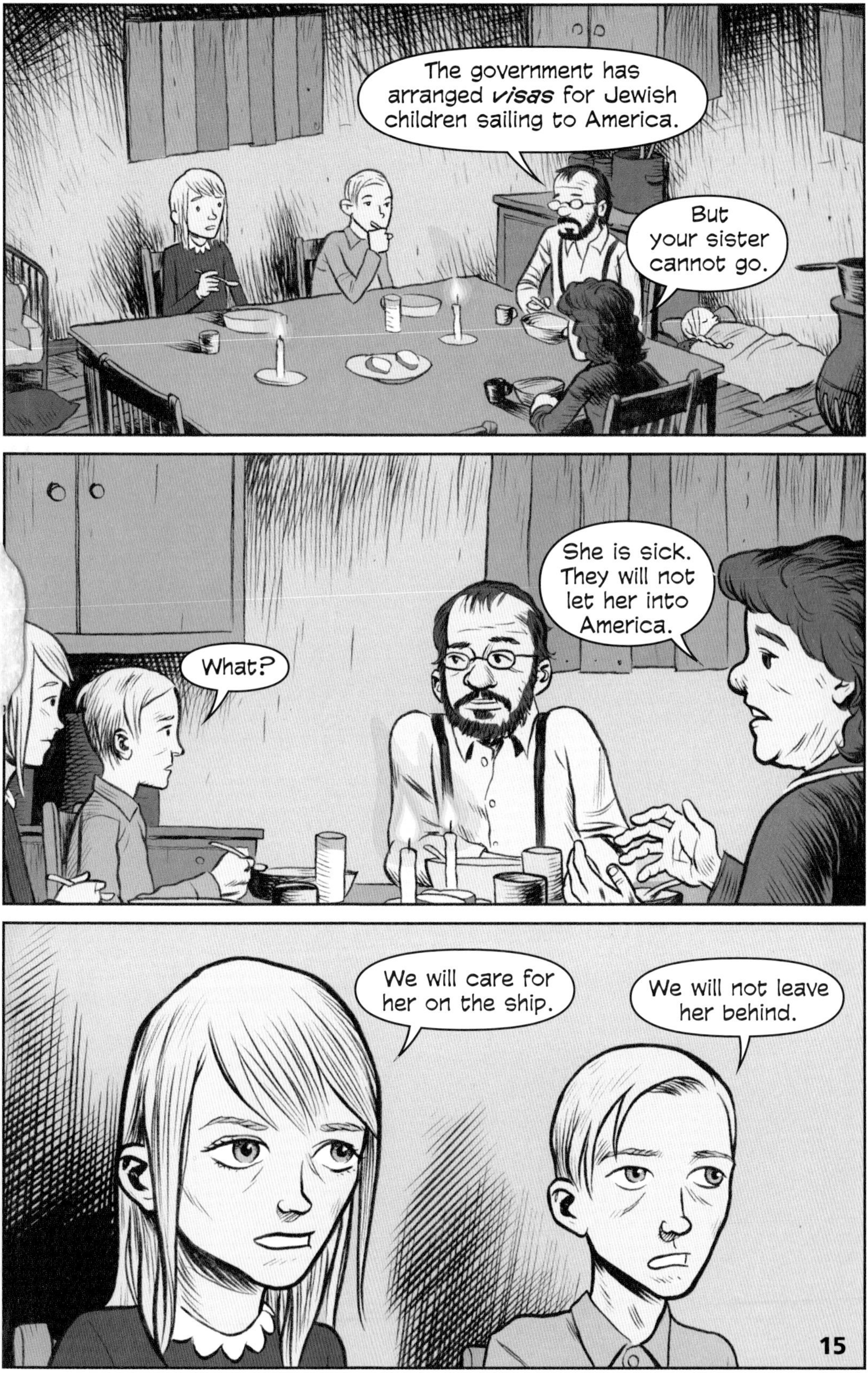
The government has arranged *visas* for Jewish children sailing to America.
But your sister cannot go.
What?
She is sick. They will not let her into America.
We will care for her on the ship.
We will not leave her behind.

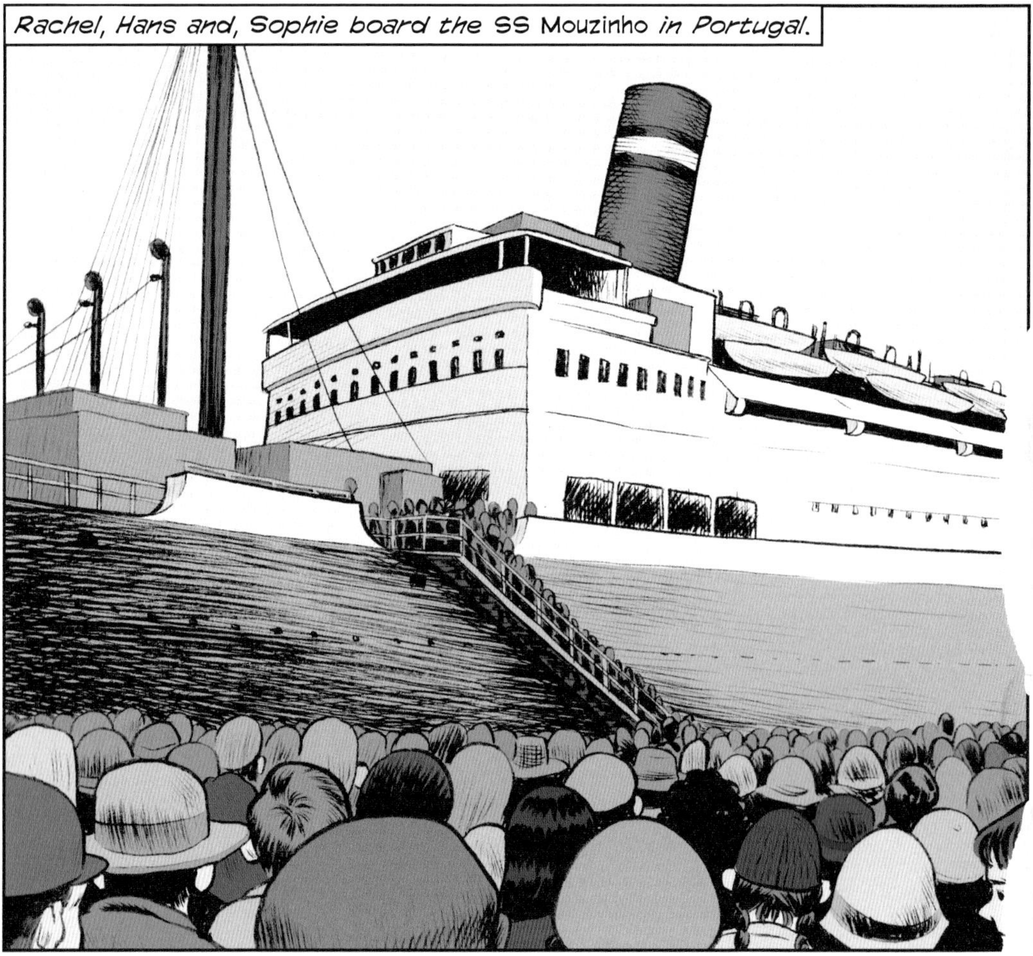
Rachel, Hans and, Sophie board the SS Mouzinho in Portugal.

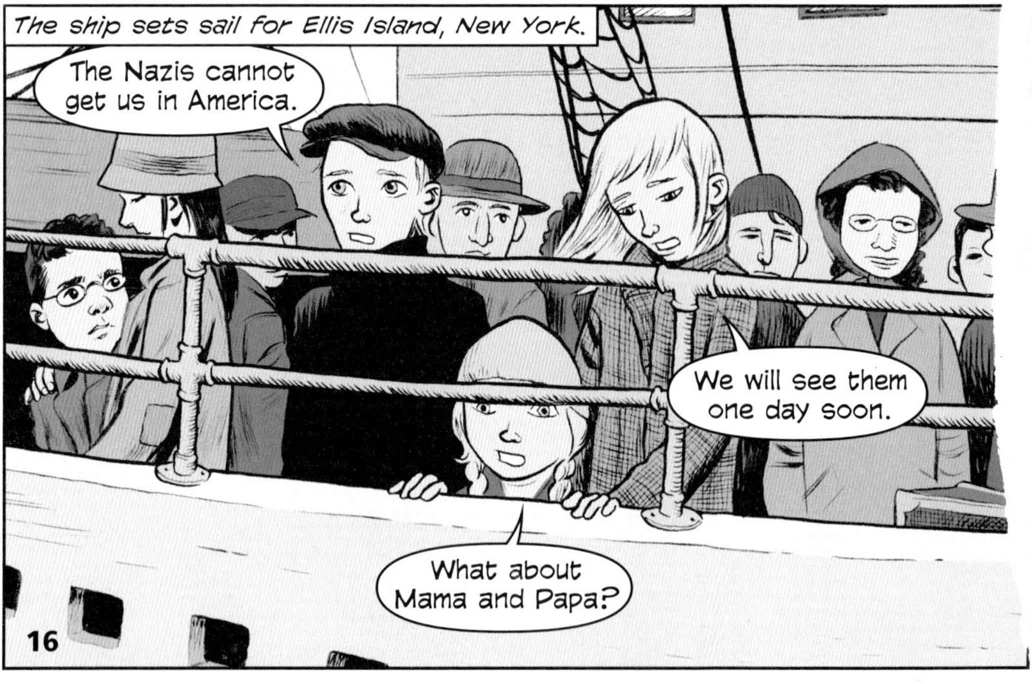
The ship sets sail for Ellis Island, New York.
The Nazis cannot get us in America.
We will see them one day soon.
What about Mama and Papa?

The *journey* took six weeks.

Many of the children are sick.

The Americans have *specified* who may enter. Sick children will be turned away.

Sophie!

We'll give her all our food.

And lots of sun.

Since official records were not kept, it is difficult to know how many Jewish refugees came to America. And for all those allowed in, many more were turned away.

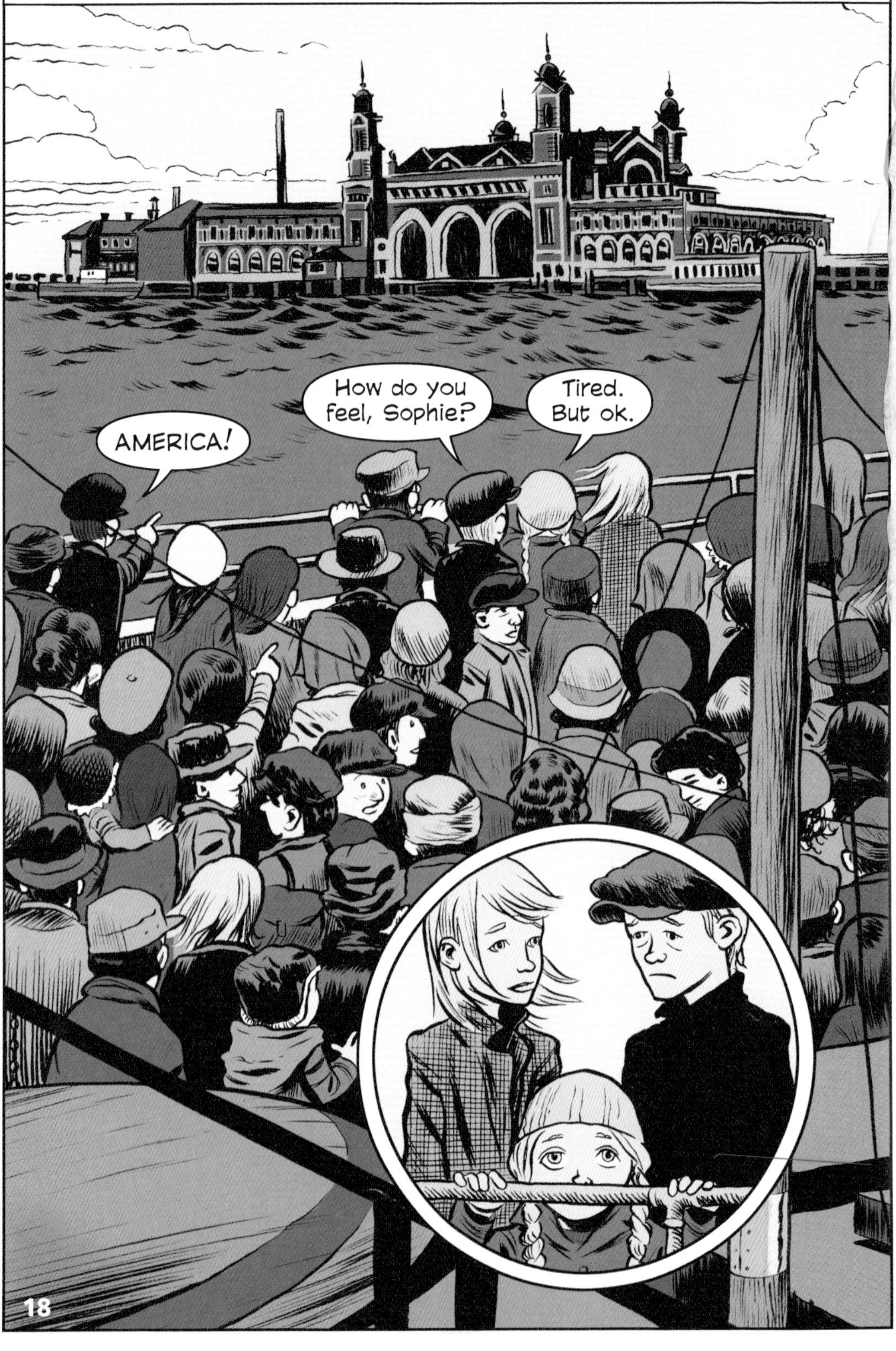
AMERICA!
How do you feel, Sophie?
Tired. But ok.

At Ellis Island, officers *examined* all children.

You do not have a visa. You must go back!

There is no one here to meet you. You cannot stay.

You did not pass the doctor's test. I'm sorry.

What if one of us is sent back?

Then we all go back.

Aunt Bette! Uncle Claude!

Rachel!

Have you heard from Papa?

We have letters from him. Your parents are well.

At least, I hope they are.

20

Wrap Up

In Nazi Germany, all Jews faced persecution. Jewish businesses and places of worship were burned. Jewish children were banned from schools. Millions of people suffered in concentration camps. Six million of them died.

My sisters and I were lucky. We escaped death with the help of several brave people. Not all Jewish children made it to safety.

There are Jewish men and women alive today who remember the Nazis. Some of them saw the horrible crimes. They were children at the time, much like me. They tell stories of great suffering, but also of hope and survival.

You'll learn about other Germans who escaped a cruel enemy in *The Rise and Fall of the Berlin Wall*. Your family members probably recall some of the events in this book.

THE RISE AND FALL OF

the Berlin Wall

John DiConsiglio

Glossary

anti-Semitic (*noun*) one who hates Jews

concentration camp (*noun*) a place where prisoners of war are held

examine (*verb*) to check or look over carefully

Gestapo (*noun*) German police force for the Nazis

invade (*verb*) to attack and take over

journey (*noun*) travel from one place to another

Nazi (*noun*) a member of the political and military group of Adolph Hitler

peasant (*noun*) a country person, like a farmer or worker in the fields

persecution (*noun*) the act of attacking someone because of who or what they are

portray (*verb*) to act like or pretend

propaganda (*noun*) written or spoken material promoting an extreme idea or opinion

safe house (*noun*) a house or apartment used as a hiding place

separate (*verb*) to split or break up

specify (*verb*) to state something in great detail

temple (*noun*) a Jewish holy place of worship

Torah (*noun*) the Jewish holy book

visa (*noun*) legal document that allows someone to travel into and within a country

worship (*noun*) honor or respect for something or someone

Idioms

keep your chin up (*page 9*) stay positive during tough times; don't look sad
"Keep your chin up. Things will get better."

old friend (*page 9*) a friend for a long time, but the person is not necessarily old
Sally is my old friend from third grade.